Compassionate Awareness

*Living Life
to
the Fullest*

Adolfo Quezada

Paulist Press
New York/Mahwah, NJ

Cover design by Sharyn Banks
Book design by Lynn Else

Library of Congress Cataloging-in-Publication Data

Quezada, Adolfo.
    Compassionate awareness : living life to the fullest / Adolfo Quezada.
        p. cm.
    ISBN 978-0-8091-4522-5 (alk. paper)
    1. Spirituality. 2. Compassion—Religious aspects—Christianity. I. Title.
    BV4501.3.Q49 2008
    248.4—dc22

                                                2007044582

Published by Paulist Press
997 Macarthur Boulevard
Mahwah, New Jersey 07430

www.paulistpress.com

Printed and bound in the United States of America

Contents

For my grandchildren: Nicholas, Alexandra,
Joshua, Alyssa, and Sommer, mystics all

Preface

...be absorbed in compassionate awareness...
—Albert Schweitzer, *Reverence for Life*, 1969

Let us be absorbed in compassionate awareness of that which is before us, for it is the life we have been given. We are the children of love, the incarnation of God. All around us we encounter the mystery of existence and we stand in awe of what we experience.

What is this state we call our life? Is it merely a dream? Will we come to know its secret? It is so fragile, and yet so vital; ethereal, yet rooted in the depths of our soul. Life, we barely know you, yet you hold us in the palm of your hand.

Elusive, unpredictable life; fulfilling, joyous life, you are pain and you are ecstasy. You span the eons that have been and are yet to be, but it is in the present moment that you manifest through us. To be absorbed in compassionate awareness means that we receive life with an open heart and tend to it one moment at a time. It means that we partake of the fruit of love and enjoy the magnificence of creation. In prayer and meditation, we receive the breath of life and transform it into the presence of God in the world.

To be absorbed in compassionate awareness of life does not mean that we cling to it. We value it above all else, yet we are prepared to lay it down for the life of another. It is when we let go of life that we are free to live it. To lose our life for the sake of love is to save it for eternity. All love emanates from God and transcends the boundaries of time and space.

As life enters into us, we enter into life, but we are not alone. In compassionate awareness, we share the human condition. We are connected to our creator and to all who have ever lived, and who are yet to live. We recognize a kindred connection with everyone and everything; a connection that cannot be severed even by death. It is a spiritual union that transcends the flesh. We are of one body. When one of us is born, we all live; when one of us is violated, we are all wounded; and when one of us is killed, we all die.

Life is but a fleeting moment on the clock of eternity, yet, it is all we have. Come, let us awaken and live life to the fullest. Let us not waste a moment of this precious time in stagnant slumber. Life is gift. In all of our wisdom, we cannot create it, yet we are responsible for it. We carry the seed of our posterity. Our love for one another evokes a compassionate awareness that sets aside discord and ends separation. We drop judgment and prejudice. We embrace all that is.

In compassionate awareness, we respect life from its inception to its conclusion. It matters not who carries the life force or for how long; every life and every moment is sacred. We share in the lives of great consequence, and we share in the lives of failure and strife. We are one with those whose lives are filled with beauty and harmony as well as with those whose lives are lost in darkness and despair.

In compassionate awareness, we respond to the desperate cries that come from the abyss of disease and starvation. We work to rehabilitate those who disrespect and disregard the lives of others. We endeavor to preserve our sacred environment and we reach out across distances and differences to promote the life that makes us one.

PART ONE

Living Mystically

CHAPTER ONE

Living Mystically

"...no one can see the kingdom of God without being born from above."   —John 3:3

Mystical living is awakened living. It is a plane of reality that is beyond the superficial nature of ordinary living. It is grounded in the belief that there is more to life than mere existence. We are open and available to the realm of spirit, yet rooted in the actuality of our human condition. Living mystically, we enter into compassionate awareness. This takes place amidst the trivial, the mundane, and the commonplace, and it is animated by the realization of a greater reality.

Jesus believed that being born into the world was not enough. He said that we must be reborn into a higher state of consciousness. Living mystically does not mean that we live in the dreams of another world more than in the reality of this one. We do not leave the world in order to find God; rather, we enter wholeheartedly into the world to discover God in everyone and everything. A mystic is simply a person who has fallen in love with the Creator and the created.

If God is the music of life, we are the instruments through which the music resounds in the universe. We are also the ears that hear the music and are attuned to it. Living mystically, we are living the life of God in the world and, at the same time, we are open to receive the bounty of creation on behalf of God.

The word *mysticism* may bring thoughts of the esoteric, of illusion, and of vague spiritual emotion. In fact, mysticism has to do with clarity, reality, and with our assimilation into the realm of God. Living mystically means that we are continually aware of being and that we allow ourselves to really experience life.

It is true that great mystics, such as St. John of the Cross and St. Teresa of Avila, have not been ordinary. They have come to a consciousness of life not developed by many. But to assume that mysticism is a state of being reserved for a small number of saintly or favored men and women is to deny the potential each one of us has for communion with God and full entry into life.

When we are living mystically we do not walk around with a smile all the time. We are not blind to the dark side of the world and the suffering of many. The difference between living mystically and living forgetfully is not in the circumstances of life, but in our response to them. Living mystically, we don't become happy when things go well for us and become unhappy when they do not. We respond with equanimity, in which we are neither happy nor sad, but openly accepting of what is without inordinate emotional response.

Living mystically, we conceptualize God less and experience the divine reality more. It is not that we don't use our intellect, but rather, that we live from the depth of our compassionate soul which is more about being than thinking. We do not seek our ultimate fulfillment, but the fulfillment of the divine will as we come to understand it. We know the divine will, not necessarily through supernatural revelations or experiences of heavenly ecstasy, but through a knowing of the heart that comes from the ultimate intimacy of prayer and meditation. When we live mystically, we allow our essence to manifest in the world. In other words, we allow God to live and love through us. We do not aim to destroy our ego, but to raise our consciousness to a level where our ego begins to serve our deeper essence.

Living mystically is living simply and honestly. We release our hold on that which inhibits authentic living. We die to the shadow self that is cast by our unfounded fears and banal desires.

We behold our own lives as they unfold before us. We notice that we are thinking, feeling, breathing, and moving. We are mindful of what is going on at the moment without judging it or trying to change it. We are aware of what is right here in front of us: the branches of a tree, the sparrow hopping on the grass, and the pen in our hand writing words.

Even as we go about our daily chores, we enter into compassionate awareness. We emulate Brother Lawrence of the Resurrection, the seventeenth-century contemplative Carmelite who, while working in the kitchen of a French monastery, dedicated his every moment to practicing the presence of God. We can be like St. Thérèse of Lisieux, the nineteenth-century Carmelite nun who brought compassion even to the smallest task. No matter whether we are brushing our teeth or sweeping the floor, driving to work or taking out the garbage, we do it consciously and compassionately.

In compassionate awareness and deep appreciation, we accept the nourishment of God. Even as we prepare what we are to eat and drink, we are conscious of the sacrifices that have been made on our behalf. The bread on our table is the fruit of life; the wine is its spirit. They are the seeds of expectation as well as the earth that incubates them. They are the warmth of the sun and the dew of the dawn. They are the labor of man and the touch of woman. In gratitude and full attention, we receive these gifts into our body that we may live for God.

We are awakened to love, forgiveness, understanding, and the divine wisdom that emanates from our deepest self. We are one with God. We are the incarnation in the world. We carry the divine energy. Every moment of our life is a breath of God. Every gesture on behalf of others, we offer in the name of God.

CHAPTER TWO

Fullness of Life

"I came that they may have life, and have it abundantly."   —John 10:10

The rebirth of our compassionate soul is like suddenly waking up from sleepwalking. We realize that we have been coming and going without being fully conscious of what we have been doing. Our mind has been very active, yet we have been virtually unconscious. Now we become conscious of what we are doing even as we do it, and observe ourselves doing it. Now we begin acting in the world instead of reacting to it.

In compassionate awareness, we cease the steady stream of thoughts that keep us preoccupied and distracted from real life. Compassionate awareness is an escape from the prison of obsession and a flight into the freedom of clarity and openheartedness. We are receptive to all that comes with life, whether pleasant or not, loveable or not, tolerable or not. We embrace what is without judgment or blame.

As we become conscious of our physicality, we awaken as if from a hypnotic state. Grounded in the reality of our body, we also awaken to the physical reality around us. We are acutely aware of the indivisibility of all that is. We stop to appreciate the uniqueness of a single tree and the intricacy of a leaf, yet we are aware that we, the tree, and the leaf are all of one essence. We know we are one with the sun, yet we are awed by its splendor at eventide.

Living mystically, we do not escape the vicissitudes of life or the physical, emotional, and spiritual pain that is part of being alive. But mystical living allows us to respond with a lucid mind and a peaceful heart.

We do not depend solely on dogma or ritual to sustain our faith, but on our actual life-experience. It is one thing to sit in church and listen to sermons about compassion, and quite another to be compassionate in the world. We will not settle for talk about God, we want to experience God.

The goal of mystical living is not ecstasy or bliss; it is to experience reality as a whole, a whole that is reflected in each part, and in which each part is precious. We can see the parts of the whole, but living mystically, we see beyond the parts to the whole.

For us, the divine essence is the basis of all that is. We realize our union with God, and consequently, we realize our union with self, others, and all of creation.

God is restful and dynamic at the same time, and is the cause and the effect of all life. In the same way, we may be invited by God to ascend the mountaintop to retreat from the hardships of life for a while, but then we are compelled by our compassionate awareness to descend into the valley of ordinary living to tend the world for God.

We understand that time is just a measure of convenience. We live in the moment because the eternal now is the only time that counts. For us, the past and the future do not exist—only the timeless present. We are conscious of the moment before us, and, whether it is a moment of ecstasy, agony, joy, or grief, we enter into it fully and experience it soberly and mindfully. We know that it is only in the moment at hand that the divine reality is revealed to us. Living mystically, we do not strive for future heavenly rewards; instead, we live believing that the realm of God is in our midst.

To cling to positive or negative circumstances is to believe in the permanence of life events. Living mystically, we cling to nothing because we believe that nothing is permanent except God. We are in the world, but not of it. We participate in life without attempting to possess it.

Because the illusion of separation is at the root of most anxiety, our belief in the oneness of all dispels that illusion. We may still be afraid of imminent threats, but our existential anxiety is diminished.

Living mystically, we are prepared to die mystically. That is, we believe our essence, which is the life of God, cannot die, but only changes in form. We are prepared to die before we die. In other words, we die moment by moment to our egoistic tendencies and fabricated self-images. We embrace both life and death. We realize that death is not an enemy to fear, but a friend to remember and to take into account with every breath. To remember the inevitability of death is to remember the preciousness of life.

CHAPTER THREE

A Desert Sermon

...I will now allure her,
and bring her into the wilderness,
and speak tenderly to her.
—Hosea 2:14

I went to church early this morning. It was not a Catholic church or a Protestant church. It wasn't a Jewish synagogue or a Muslim mosque. In fact, it wasn't a building belonging to any religious organization. It was God's church. It was the desert.

How beautifully decorated it was. The mesquites glistened with morning dew, the *Cholla cacti,* each unique unto itself, offered attention and respect, and the Palo Verde trees, with roots firmly planted in the earth, reached for the heavens in humble petition.

It was still quiet and the sparrows and mockingbirds had barely begun their morning prayers. I noticed several young jackrabbits in the brush and I assumed they had come to share the solemn occasion. I was wrong. They began to romp and play. It was plain that they did not want to contemplate with me the beauty of God's nature; they wanted to be the beauty of God's nature.

Then the high priest arrived atop a Palo Verde tree. It was a hummingbird. She wore no elaborate robes, just her luminescent feathers that reflected the hues of the rising sun. There was little ritual, but she stayed long enough to deliver a sermon that I needed to hear.

When we think of a hummingbird, we envision a little bird with a long beak that flaps its wings at what seems a million times a second. It bolts to and fro, constantly on the move, working to retrieve nectar from flowers, and never stops long enough to catch its breath.

But this hummingbird sat on the uppermost branch of her green altar, singing praises with music that sounded like no other bird. Here she sat, not frantically flapping her wings, but being still.

Her message to me was this: "It is true that I move about at high speeds and work and play with such vigor that I use much energy. Yet, I too must stop and rest frequently to restore myself. I too must land and come to terms with who I am and what I'm doing here. I too must look to the source of my energy and allow myself to be recharged before I fly again. Stop and rest and be made whole again before you continue your journey."

By now the eastern skies were turning purple and pink. The sun continued rising through horizontal clouds. I could see the hummingbird more clearly. She was small. How awesome that all that energy and all that music were coming from such a little one.

She said to me: "I am small, I am limited, and I am dependent on the Creator for all that I am and all that I do. I am small, but the spirit within me transcends the cosmos. Embracing my littleness, I release my hold on the illusion of power and control. I discover that my only task is to be true to myself and to be who I am, nothing more, nothing less. Recognize your smallness and you will manifest the largesse of creation."

The hummingbird suddenly shot up into the air like an ascending spirit and then dove toward the ground like a missile. Only feet above the ground she broke her dive, uttering a sharp chirp and then soared up again, repeating this antic several times. She didn't ask for more than to be allowed to sing, to play, to work, and to fly.

She said: "Be simple. Let go of all that is not yours to have. Be satisfied and grateful for the simple gifts that are granted and use them well. Be realistic in your expectations, lest you demand more of yourself than does the Creator."

Then the hummingbird bade me farewell until another day and flew across the desert sky until I could see her no more. But I will see her again and be reminded to stop, to be small, and to be simple. I will return to the desert and there I will watch, listen, and learn.

CHAPTER FOUR

Watch and Pray

"Stay awake and pray..."
—Matthew 26:41

C ompassion is something we are, not something we do; yet, there is something we must
do in order to allow our natural state of compassion to arise. We must become still, silent, and
single hearted. Compassion is not an emotion or an
energy that we turn on and off at will. It is the natural, mystical state of our soul. The problem is that
we are not aware of that state unless we stop and
turn within ourselves.

In prayer and meditation we are compassionately present with God, that is, we are open, available, attentive, and totally involved with the divine.
Both the Old Testament and the New Testament ask
believers to love God with all their heart, all their
mind, all their soul, and all their strength (Deut 6:4;
Mark 12:30). When we unite with God this intimately, we are not only loving God, we are living
God.

We do not abandon the circumstances in which we live. On the contrary, in compassionate awareness, we are compelled by the love of God to stay and tend to the wounds of our brothers and sisters, and to work with a single-minded purpose for harmony between our inner and outer worlds.

When we are living mystically, we pray and meditate with all of our senses. We do not deny the physical; rather, our senses are quickened to experience life to the fullest. In prayer and meditation, we become silent that we may hear, we go blind that we may see, and we empty ourselves that we may receive.

In prayer and meditation, we stop and listen, we breathe and notice. In this attentiveness to the moment before us, we come alive. At this point of inner clarity our essence manifests. It is God. Thoughts only get in the way. Even our emotions block the light that emanates from our compassionate soul. This is not a time of power, knowledge, or possession. It is a time of no dimension; it is the eternal now.

In prayer and meditation, we allow our mind to settle, dropping away distracting thoughts, and focusing our attention on what is before us at the moment. "...[R]emain here, and stay awake with me" (Matt 26:38). God would have us leave whatever we are doing and postpone whatever we have planned to remain and stay awake in prayer and meditation. From this hour with God comes the strength, courage, and perseverance that are needed in the hour of trial and tribulation. "…[D]o not fear, for I am with you, do not be afraid, for I am your God" (Isa 41:10).

It is good that we stop on occasion to pray for the welfare of others. There is a mysterious and mystical energy that moves in the world when we do. Yet, compassion is more than this. It permeates our existence with a constant aspiration for the well-being of others. It is a prayer without words, without specifics, and without ceasing. Because in the overall scheme of things, we don't really know what is best for others, in prayer we just hold them in our heart. In this prayer of compassionate awareness, we are one with them.

In the depth of our prayer and meditation, the illusion of duality falls away and we come to realize that there is no I and God, but only I AM. Connection, bonding, integration, and even communion happen between two or more beings, but we have always been one with God. All that is, exists in us, and we are a part of all existence.

When we pray and meditate, we become conscious of our oneness with God, but in addition, we become aware of our oneness with all who live, have lived, or ever will live. Being with God is being with all. The energy that is within every living creature is the same energy that dwells within our being. In our attention to all that is, we touch the essence of God.

At the deepest place within ourselves we discover our divinity. Here we encounter boundless compassion and complete acceptance. Here there is an abundance of care and attention for the universe and for all that is a part of it. In this divine compassion, we find that not a single quark is unaccounted for, and nary a detail is overlooked. All is precious in the eyes of God; each part as important as the next. We see the suffering world through the eyes of God and we cry the tears of God. We share the wounds of the world and feel God's compassion moving in and through us. God ignites the fire of conscious love in our soul, and animates our acts of loving kindness in the world.

It was on a cold winter morning that I stopped at a nearby church. I like to go there early before anybody else arrives. It is one of the few churches that leaves its doors open through the night.

What a glorious experience to sit in silence and pray in such a way that we may carry the presence of God with us throughout the day. On this occasion, I entered the warmth of the church only to find that my place of prayer, my haven of peace, my temple of tranquility, had been invaded by a transient. It seems this man had no place to lay his head and decided to take refuge from the cold night air in the church. He was all curled up in the corner of the area that I had claimed as my domain.

My immediate reaction was to become angry with him. Although I didn't wake him, I thought, "How dare you take my space! Don't you know how important it is for me to be there to pray?" Then it hit me. How ridiculous to think my prayer time was more important than the plight of this man. How insensitive of me to place my so-called spiritual needs before his obvious physical needs. How presumptuous of me to consider this chapel, which we call the house of God, as anything less than a sanctuary for all humanity.

As I withdrew quietly into the darkness of the early morning, I realized I had placed praying about life above life itself. I asked forgiveness from God and from the man on the floor.

Maybe I could not lift this man from his poverty, but at least I could commend him to God and not disturb his sleep. Actually, this man had not really kept me from praying. He had given me a reason to pray. Yet, even as I walked and prayed for the transient and for those who live with the pain of poverty, I could already feel that prayer wasn't enough. Prayer is indeed an intimate affair, but real prayer takes us out of ourselves unto our brothers and sisters.

It seems that just as we get cozy and secure with our prayer life, we are quickly and bluntly reminded that we are not to use our communion with God as opium that desensitizes us from the pain of living. Rather, prayer and meditation open us up to love and compassion. They sensitize us to feel not only our own pain, but also the pain of others. Rather than take us away from the squalor of the world, prayer and meditation throw us into the center of it. The peace we seek through prayer and meditation is not a peace of tranquility, but a peace of truthfulness. In light of this truth, we cannot ignore the condition of our brothers and sisters or neglect our responsibility to bring them some relief. When we pray and meditate, the power of God's compassion is released through us into the world.

I Came to Pray

I came to pray in solitude in hope of peace and calm, but I was not allowed escape into a blissful state. Instead, I stayed with my ground of being, and the reality of life. Here I saw the pain of others, and the suffering of the world.

I came to pray to soar with angels at ecstatic heights, but I was sorely disappointed that I could not take flight. Instead, I was brought down by mourning for the dying and the dead. I saw those who were hurting, and the victims of abuse.

I came to pray in union with the heart of God, but I was sent to squalid places, not at all what I had sought. Instead, I saw the starving children in a country far away, and the bones of youthful soldiers sent by those who honor war.

I came to pray for the power of faith and the strength of hope that I might help the powerless, the weak, and the vulnerable, but this was not to be. Instead, I was left powerless with the powerless, weak with the weak, and vulnerable with the vulnerable.

I came to pray for inspiration, holiness, and grace, but I was given even more. Instead, my heart filled with compassion for every soul on earth. I felt their pain and lived their poverty, I grieved and cried for every loss. And now, I come to pray to mostly listen and obey.

CHAPTER FIVE

One with God

"...I am in my Father, and you in me, and I in you..."   —John 14:20

Go transcends humanity, yet is immanent with it. Because we are in God and God is in us, our life is one way in which God's love and compassion are made known to others. And, although we cannot even begin to comprehend the ineffable and incomprehensible nature of God, we allow God's nature, which we share, to manifest in the world through us.

Jesus understood the union between God and humanity. He believed in the oneness of all and warned against the illusion of separation. He taught that in union there was life and strength, but in dispersion there was lifelessness and impotence.

As we begin life, oneness is our only reality. In the union of infant and mother, we know no separation at the level of the soul. It is at this level that we discover our truest nature. At the depth of our essence we are not unto ourselves. Our essence belongs to God as does the essence of every living being. This means that we are all of one essence. This oneness that we experience is our most natural state. It was our reality before we were born into this world and it will be our reality after we leave it. This oneness, of which we are an integral part, transcends both life and death. Gradually we develop our individuality and sense of separateness from our mother. This is essential for healthy maturation. But unless we remain connected to the whole at a deeper level, we become isolated and overly self-sufficient.

If we are to be saved from internal and external disintegration, we must be reminded regularly of our intrinsic connection to all that is. Nature reminds us of this, so does silence and solitude, prayer and meditation. Sometimes the reminder comes to us abruptly when we have wandered off into the far country and become lost. Then we remember and make our return.

In compassionate awareness, we live a seamless existence with God. Nothing we think or do is outside of God. We walk, talk, play, and work in God-consciousness. Whether we are engaged in prayer and meditation or polishing our shoes, we are conscious of God. In this selfless state of mind and heart, we realize that divine compassion does not enter us, rather, we enter divine compassion. We live out the ordinariness of our humanity aware of our divinity, and we live out the extraordinariness of our divinity aware of our humanity. Our humanity and our divinity are two natures in one being.

God is in the universe, but is not the universe. God is in the world, but is not the world. God is in us, but is not us. The universe, the world, and we are in God, but we are not God. This is the paradox: we are distinct beings and, at the same time, we are one with God. So prayer and meditation are not ways of connecting or communing with God, but ways of becoming aware of our oneness with the divine that has always been and will forever be. In compassionate awareness, we go beyond mere identification with the divine to inclusiveness. To experience hell is to fall into the illusion of separation from God.

In the midst of our own agony and despair, we can feel very alone. Yet, when we go within to pray and meditate we discover that we are not alone at all. At the core of our shattered self we become aware of God's compassion. This means that God is with us in our darkest hour, giving us the strength and courage to make it through the night. But that is not all. We also become aware of the compassion of others, known and unknown, who hold us in their hearts, not necessarily to rescue us from our suffering, but to accompany us as we move through it.

Compassion is another name for God, yet sometimes we wonder why God's compassion allows disasters of major proportion to happen to creation. Maybe nobody believes any longer that God is wrathful and reigns terror on us when we don't behave. But some of us still look to God to prevent natural and man-made disasters from happening to us.

Recently our world has experienced a series of disasters that have overwhelmed our capacity to respond. From these disasters we have learned that we must prepare for more to come, and that we must work together if we are to survive. Our earth has been rocked by earthquakes, tsunamis, floods, hurricanes, fires, and terrorism.

I remember one earthquake in particular. The whole world began to tremble, the ground came apart, buildings toppled, and highways and bridges collapsed. Hundreds of people in San Francisco were killed, thousands were injured, and many were left homeless. It was as if the Apocalypse had come for those caught in this earthquake.

How could this or any other natural catastrophe happen to innocent people when there is supposed to be a compassionate God? Where was God's compassion when the concrete blocks were falling on top of helpless children? Where was God's compassion when the walls crushed elderly persons? Where was God's compassion when so many were left without shelter? There was chaos and confusion, death and destruction all around. Where was God's compassion?

Natural disasters are the dynamic of the nature in which we live. When bad things happen, God is compassionately with us as we deal with them. It is God who gives us the courage, the strength, and the wherewithal to cope in the best way we can with the worst that can happen.

Where was God's compassion when the earthquake hit? It was manifested in the loving action taken by so many in the midst of the disaster. There was the fifty-two-year-old African-American man who left his home to help save fourteen people, most of them white. Where was God's compassion? It was in each of the three hundred off-duty firefighters who turned up in full gear within two hours of the earthquake. It was in the store officials who decided to give away bottles of water to quake victims whose water would be turned off for days. It was in the engineers who kept working even after rescue efforts had officially been suspended because of bad weather and dangerous conditions. Their sixty hours of work resulted in the rescue of a fifty-seven-year-old man who had been buried alive for ninety hours in the wreckage of his car.

Where was God's compassion? It was in the residents who saw that water needed to be pumped from the bay to fight the fires, and carried hoses through the streets to help. It was in the electricians and carpenters who voluntarily showed up at dawn to shore up buildings, freeing firefighters to search for survivors. It was in the doctors who worked many hours to rescue a six-year-old boy and his eight-year-old sister from the wreckage of their family car. It was in the more than five hundred people who mailed in thousands of dollars to help those children.

Where was God's compassion? It was in the residents of what is known as a crack- and crime-infested neighborhood, who within minutes of the quake ran out with pliers, car jacks, flashlights, and ladders to begin rescuing survivors. It was in the doctors who were operating on a sixty-five-year-old man when the quake hit. In complete disregard for their own safety, they quickly threw themselves over their patient to protect him from falling objects.

Where was God's compassion? It was in each of the many ordinary citizens who rushed into action the moment they knew others were in trouble. Where was God's compassion? It was there in the form of the men and women who took compassionate action on behalf of others. They were one with God.

CHAPTER SIX

One with Ourselves

The part can never be well unless the whole is
well.   —Socrates (in Plato's *Charmides*)

Yesterday as I walked through the desert, I
watched the sky. It was beautiful at eventide.
It seemed as though there was balance in the
cosmos, synergy in the universe, and justice in the
world. To the west the sun shone bright and orange,
not yet ready to take its leave. To the east the moon
was full and white and wonderful, not competing,
but completing the heavenly scene. It was the marriage of the sun and the moon—the union of the
parts.

Once all we knew was unity and wholeness.
All was one, there was no other. Then came the separation, and we were thrown into a world of duality.
Now there is within and without, conscious and
unconscious, up and down, good and evil, mascu-
line and feminine, soul and spirit. But our goal is
neither to do away with the duality nor to integrate
the opposites. Instead, it is a time for the marriage

of opposites; a marriage that respects and maintains the uniqueness of each, yet allows the interdependence of both. Our wholeness comes even as we embrace our multiplicity.

At our core, we are whole. In the light of God, we are at one with ourselves. As whole beings, we recognize and accept the many selves within us. We respect their differences and appreciate the contribution each part of us plays in our life. We are not any one of our parts, but the sum total of them all. We do not set up a war between our higher and lower natures, or between the powers of light and darkness within us. Instead, we embrace even those parts of us that offend, and allow the peace of love to touch all the natures, all the levels, and all the colors within.

In compassionate awareness, we take back the shadow parts we have disowned. We find that often the most unwanted parts of us end up as the most creative and valuable. We come to know all of our parts, including those we consider dark, animalistic, and primordial. We come to understand those parts and learn what their needs are, then we respond to the various parts in healthy ways before they grow out of control and attempt to meet their needs in unhealthy and counterproductive ways.

As we move toward wholeness, we can see the nature of our creativeness as well as our destructiveness. We see how gentle we can be—and how aggressive. In the mirror of the soul, we are faced with our lightness of being as well as with our dark side. Here nothing is hidden, and nothing is judged. Our compassionate soul does not choose between the good and evil in us, and it does not select the beautiful and leave behind the ugly. Our many parts come together in the acceptance of love.

As we move toward oneness with ourselves, the energies of our body, mind, and soul converge. We sense that our body needs to be touched, fed, and exercised. We know that our mind must be taught, stretched intellectually, and challenged creatively. We believe in the ability of our soul to soar with the angels and penetrate the depths of spiritual mysteries. As we tend to each of these parts, we tend to the whole.

Our internal oneness is the consequence of our prayer and meditation. We stop to give rest to the parts and to allow them to consolidate. We examine our external life to ensure its congruence with our inner life.

The rhythm of our life is giving and receiving, and the balance of the two is the way of creation. First we open to the seed, the rain, and the sun before we can offer up the fruit. We are earth and water, fire and air. We are matter and we are spirit. We destroy and we give life. We die to the old and are born to the new. Life and death complete our oneness.

CHAPTER SEVEN

One with Creation

"...unless you change and become like children,
you will never enter the kingdom of heaven."
—Matthew 18:3

Jesus referred to the nature of children as one
belonging to all of us, regardless of our age, but
which we abandon as we grow older. He called
his disciples to that glorious state of mind in which
all is new and mysterious and every event is an
exciting adventure. He knew that life is yet a wonder to children, hence their reverence for everything
about it.

We change and become like children when
we allow ourselves to be recipients of what others
offer, and when we set aside our pretentious self-
sufficiency. We settle into our own simplicity and
stop living according to public opinion. We drop
our defensiveness and confess to ourselves and to
each other our vulnerability. The child within us
sees life with a special clarity, unpolluted by suspi-
cions, ambitions, insecurities and prejudices.

In compassionate awareness, we come to life as a child—full of awe and wonderment. A child is enthralled with the berries on a bush and the descent of a dancing snowflake. A child is totally involved with a ladybug and focused on the shape of a twig. A child is open to full experience.

Mystics are in love with God and with life. To become like children is to enter the realm of mystical living. Children are naturally mystics. My five-year-old granddaughter, Sommer, is such a mystic. It's not just because she's innocent, but because she is unadulterated by the need to control life through analyses and classification. She is still simple. Even at two years of life I witnessed the animation of her compassionate soul. Her big, bright eyes captured everything in their scope. She focused on the butterfly as it fluttered to and fro. She studied the ants as they went about their work. She especially loved the multicolored flowers that she could touch. Sound was important to her as well. She could hear a dog barking in the distance and the unseen helicopter above.

How glorious is the world through the eyes and ears of a child. How abundant is the bounty a child enjoys. How precious is this childhood season when life is now and all is here. It is a time of innocence, a time of sweet surrender to what is.

When we identify ourselves by the things we accumulate, we are living from an ego state that has no foundation in truth. When we identify ourselves with the things that surround us, we are living from a state that knows no separation from all that is.

Living mystically, we awaken to the reality that everything that has been called into existence is interrelated in one universe. The parts of the whole affect one another. No one part of the universe stands independently of the others. In fact, the whole is present in each and every part. It seems that nothing stands separate and alone. We depend on the earth, the earth depends on the sun, the sun depends on the universe, and on it goes. The reality of this utter dependence at all levels of existence explodes any illusion of isolation.

In compassionate awareness, we remain open to all that life presents to us, including the magnificence of nature. We are in awe of majestic mountain peaks that commune with the heavens. We are in wonderment as we behold the beauty and grace of a tiny hummingbird. We lose any illusion of separateness as we gaze at the plethora of heavenly bodies in the midnight sky. All is one and one is all. Everything, whether animate or inanimate, is imbued with divine essence. As such, it exacts our utmost attention and consideration.

When we are in compassionate awareness with nature, we enter the ecstasy of just being for the glory of God. The clouds and the rains, the streams and the oceans exist just to be. The squirrels and the bees, the snakes and the coyotes image the beauty of God. We are one with all creation in its delight and in its torment. And when the precious gifts of nature are violated and destroyed, we are equally violated and destroyed. Recently, I found myself feeling compassion for two giant *Saguaro cacti* that were hewn down by ax-wielding vandals. My compassion for the cacti stayed with me for quite a while. Then my compassion expanded to include the vandals. They must be miserable within, I thought, to have acted out in such a hateful and violent manner.

In compassionate awareness, our attention is drawn, not to the loud and ostentatious, but to the natural. Through the eyes of compassion we see everything as beautiful and valuable. We revere the sacred that is found everywhere we turn.

We allow the world around us to be what it is and we enter into it. We move from a relationship of the observer and the observed to the intimacy of one. We come to respect what is. Persons and things are who and what they are, not what we need them to be.

Rocks on the ground are of many-splendored colors. Each is unique in shape and composition; each has its own story to tell. The trees are life itself. There is hope and there is faith in those dark and brittle limbs. We can hear the chirp of the hummingbird only if we really listen. There is so much noise, but it is not the noise of the city. It is the noise inside our head. We quiet the noise and let the song of life serenade us through creation. "Do you have eyes, and fail to see? Do you have ears, and fail to hear?" (Mark 8:18).

CHAPTER EIGHT

One with Others

...we who are many are one body.
—1 Corinthians 10:17

God has many faces, yet, there is but one God, and the essence of God is in every single person. There is such diversity in our world, yet all of it emerging from one God. We are a mosaic of unique and varied beings, a humanity held in the unity of God. The form others take in our perception of them may be illusion, but our integrality with them is not.

There is within each of us a basic hunger for union with the rest of humanity, an urge to transcend race, religion, age, socioeconomic status, and even the lifetimes that lie between us. We live from day to day separately and on a mundane level, yet there is something that draws us together on a higher plane.

We are a paradox in that we desire so much to be autonomous, free, independent, and individually identified, and, at the same time, we hunger for the peace and harmony of soul that come only of union with others. What is this instinctual pull that has us gravitating toward the whole, re-membering ourselves to the one body to which we have always belonged? It is love: love for God, love for ourselves, and love for each other.

Compassionate awareness is our primordial sense of oneness with all that is, especially our fellow human beings. Compassion is hard-wired into our humanity. We actually have to be taught about separation and conditioned into apathy. As long as we believe that we are beings unto ourselves, separate from others, we cannot enter into compassionate awareness.

We are one another at our core. There is no I and thou. Whatever illusion of separation we may be clinging to falls away in compassionate awareness, leaving only the reality of oneness. This alleviates suffering because much of suffering comes about as a result of the illusion of separation.

When we are with another person in compassionate awareness, we remember that, at some level, we and the other person are not two, but one. It is a mystical state in which the walls of separation fall away and the illusion of the isolated self dissolves. We realize that what happens to one happens to the other and vice versa. In fact, we feel the pain of the whole world because the suffering of one is the suffering of all.

We are called not merely to compassion, but to radical compassion; the kind of compassion that knocks down the barriers that separate us from one another and, with great respect for uniqueness and diversity, embraces the unity that is our reality.

When we are living mystically and loving consciously, we realize that we are the wave that is also the ocean. But in our journey toward the whole, we encounter a tremendous fear of nonexistence. We believe that becoming part of the whole may mean our annihilation. This existential anxiety has us scurrying back to our isolated cells, as if by proclaiming our separateness we could ensure our perpetuity. When we allow love to take us out of ourselves through compassionate awareness, we no longer fear nonexistence, and we enter into the highest existence of all.

Recognizing our oneness with others does not mean that we give up our uniqueness and individuality. It means that we appreciate who we are and develop ourselves to our full potential. Our growth as individuals leads us to a state that goes beyond the self. What has been important to us still is, yet, we come to discover more universal considerations as we mature spiritually. We behold a bigger picture than when we began.

Whereas before we preferred to be special and above the rest, now we seek union in the humility of equality. Whereas before we held dearly to our separated selves as a sign of who we were, now we welcome union, not as the death of our being, but as the birth of our truest self.

Unity does not preclude the necessary development of individual egos and distinct personalities. But once our ego is solidly established in our early years of life, we begin to balance it with the world beyond ourselves. We learn that just as we have feelings, others do too. We learn that we can empathize with the emotions of others and sometimes even understand them. We discover the commonalities we share with others. We look upon the differences of others with respect, appreciation, and a willingness to learn and grow from them. This is compassionate awareness.

Sometimes we are afraid of those who are different from us and we stay away from those we don't understand. But our attachment or aversion to certain persons or things fades away in the light of conscious loving. Compassionate awareness compels us to release that to which we cling and to embrace that which we push away. It takes us beyond any preconceived notions we may have, and transcends any boundaries we may have arbitrarily set for ourselves or others. Compassionate awareness leaves behind assumptions and sets aside expectations. It breaks through the constriction of prejudice.

Generally, the way we treat others is contingent on whether or not we identify with them. Toward those with whom we can relate, we are kinder and gentler. Toward those who seem different from us, we are more distant and apathetic. It is only when we find the common denomination between ourselves and others that we feel compassion for them and desire their welfare. Compassionate awareness is blind to external considerations. Compassion is energy of the heart that moves toward one and all because it assumes that we are one with all.

When we judge others or hold them in contempt, we have to do it from a distance. We cannot have compassion on them and, at the same time, hate or envy them. Only by leaving compassionate awareness and entering into the illusion of separation can we stand against others.

When we realize that we are all of one body, all born from the same source, we cease our fear of one another and close the distance between us. · Compassionate awareness necessitates closeness. It is one thing to be compassionate toward someone we love and quite another to feel compassion toward strangers. But the realization of the oneness we share, even with strangers, provides the intimacy of spirit that opens us to compassion. When one person is compassionately present to another, the energy that is generated between them transcends their relationship and impacts on the world.

In compassionate awareness, we are not compassionate toward one person in dire circumstances and not toward another in the same circumstances. Compassion requires respect and does not distinguish between the lovable or unlovable, oppressed or oppressor, friend or enemy. All are equal in the light of compassion.

Being one with others in compassionate awareness includes being one with those who lie and steal, kill and rape. Our compassion takes us into the world of the mentally sick, the apathetic, the mean, and those we consider evil. Loving consciously, we are one with the demons as well as the angels. It matters not that some oppose us or aim to end our life; the foes who would destroy us don't know that we are them. In compassionate awareness, we embrace the oneness of all, and even our enemies abide in our heart. "The Lord is good to all, and his compassion is over all that he has made" (Ps 145:9).

Compassion is an intimate experience because it involves seeing through the eyes of others, feeling what they feel, and thinking what they think. Nothing is more intimate than the oneness of compassion. In compassionate awareness, we bring more than empathy and understanding to a relationship. Because all compassion emanates from the divine, when we penetrate a relationship with compassion, we evoke the essence of the divine.

I Am You

My heart is moved as I behold the world, so much suffering, so much pain. Everywhere I turn there is misery and strife. Wounded world, I am not separate from you. Your hurt is my hurt; your anguish is mine.

In my compassion I become one with the world. I feel its pulse and enter into its passion.

I am you, little girl, who was left stranded in the killing fields without a mother, without a chance of life.

I am you, mother of small ones, who alone must face a hard and uncertain life.

I am you, woman, who is cursed with a disintegrating body with little hope for cure.

I am you, man of middle years, who carries the burden of the world on your shoulders and would rather die than go on like this.

I am you, young boy, who has been sexually assaulted by a priest.

I am you, priest, who is accused of abusing children.

I am you, who are hungry, needy, and poor.

I am you, who are imprisoned by the bars of addiction, the fear of living, or the circumstances of your life.

I am you, who feel helpless, hopeless, and faithless.

I am you, who are lost, confused, and purposeless.

I am you, who are lonely, sad, and depressed.

I am you, and you are me.

PART TWO

Loving
Consciously

CHAPTER NINE

Loving Consciously

"Just as I have loved you, you also should love one another." —John 13:34

A flower is of God. As a seed, it dies into the darkness of the earth before bringing forth new life. First it incubates and gestates, and then it sprouts into a seedling. As it struggles through the alimented mud, it searches for the light. Rooted in the ground of being and open to the rains of heaven, it grows in strength and the wisdom of nature. Suddenly it blossoms forth in grace and beauty, not to be of the world, but to be in the world; not to be impressive, but because that is its true nature. In the same way, we must die to our distracted self and allow the rebirth of our compassionate soul. In prayer and meditation, we remember that we too are of God. We are not here to react to life; we are life. We are not here to love; we are love.

Love is at the core of compassionate awareness. We cannot love without being moved by compassion and we cannot feel compassion without knowing love. This is not a sentimental or romantic love that wants its own way, but a universal love that reaches beyond the self for the good of all. Because compassionate awareness is rooted in love, it manifests in loving kindness and open heartedness toward ourselves and others.

No religion or spiritual tradition has a monopoly on compassion. In fact, compassion is one of the main tenets of Christianity, Buddhism, Judaism, Islam, and other religions. Compassion transcends the boundaries of religion and supersedes the doctrines and dogma of people. It is a basic human impulse, a uniquely human quality, a capacity that is inherent to our nature as beings of God. It is the power of the heart that prompts us to be with others in nonjudgmental, merciful, kind, forgiving, patient, accepting, and understanding ways. It is the energy of love that moves through us and toward others, the force that compels us to act on behalf of those in need. It is not an acquired skill, but an intrinsic ability that needs only to be awakened.

Compassion overwhelms apathy and animates the soul. It may prompt a heartfelt tear or it may change the course of history. It may prompt a gentle gesture or it may inspire the sacrifice of life.

We may be moved to compassion by the circumstances before us, such as a hungry child, but compassion is not created by circumstances. It is not a reaction to life; rather, it is a way of life. Our compassion is there even before we encounter the hungry child. The circumstances before us merely evoke our compassionate soul.

Compassion does not require a certain set of circumstances or a special atmosphere in which to make its appearance. It comes in the midst of a storm despite the chaos and stress. It comes in the midst of calm despite order and tranquility. Even when circumstances are such that all seems lost, compassion is still possible. Nothing can stop compassion except our decision to leave the awareness of the present moment.

Although compassion is our natural state, our conditioned state is too often one of distraction. Like any of our God-given attributes, compassion can atrophy through lack of use. We can also become emotionally calloused by an environment that bombards us with violence and killing in the name of entertainment. All the while, we are called back to compassionate awareness and conscious loving.

Compassion is about touching—not necessarily physical touching—but the touching of hearts and minds. We are touched by the plight of others and are moved to compassionate action. Broken bodies are treated gently and patiently as they mend. Broken hearts are allowed to grieve their losses and lament their mistakes. Broken minds are listened to, given clarity, and offered inspiration. Just as God shares our joys and sorrows, our life and death, so do we share the lives of others along with their burdens and their delights. Our compassion is the touch of God. It has the power to heal.

Compassion is the nectar with which we nurture and nourish the world, but before we can share from our cup of compassion, we must first fill it with compassion for ourselves. When we are open and attentive to our own life, including the suffering and joy that come our way, then we can be open and attentive to the lives of others.

Our sense of connectedness with all that is begins with our sense of connectedness within ourselves. When we feel a connection between our body, mind, and spirit, we are better able to stay conscious of the moment before us.

Although it is important that we not allow our own set of circumstances to blind us to the problems of others, it is equally as important that we not allow the suffering of others to blind us to our own suffering. Our temptation in the face of suffering is to distract ourselves from it somehow. In compassion, however, we stay aware of our suffering and enter fully into the experience. We can put our own problems into perspective in relation to the problems of others, as long as we do not discount ourselves in the process.

In compassion, our goal is not to feel good or peaceful, but to be real, whatever we may be feeling. We stay with our emotions, whatever they may be, without judging them.

When sorrow is upon us, compassion compels us to let the sorrow penetrate the walls that we have built to keep out emotions. Compassion lets the sorrow touch our heart and be fully experienced. Only then can we respond to life with our whole self. To be able to feel the feelings of others, we must first be willing and able to feel our own.

In compassion, we protect ourselves from any harmful environment or mistreatment. We are aware of our physicality and tend to the true needs of our body. We do not behave in ways that are detrimental to ourselves. We identify the person, place, or thing that is the root of our suffering and we let it go.

If we were fortunate enough to have had tender, caring parents, we were probably held by them compassionately whenever we were hurt in some way. Being held was all we needed to endure the pain and to not despair. As adults, we must be the ones who hold ourselves tenderly along with our hurting bodies and broken hearts. We stay with ourselves even through the times of affliction, remembering all the while that it is we who carry the compassion of God to the world, including to ourselves.

Our compassion for others is manifested through action, but in our enthusiasm to respond to their needs, we are in danger of straying too far from the source of all compassion. Compassion compels us to respond to the cries of a world that is hurting, hungering, and searching for life. It inspires us to use the talents we have been given to nurture, feed, and guide our brothers and sisters, but sometimes we forget that we can do only that which we are empowered to do by the source of all power.

When our response to the needs of others is pulled from us by the gravity of those needs, we quickly lose the power to respond at all. Anything that comes from us must be the fruit of a vine well planted in the soil of prayer and meditation, and nurtured to fruition by the warmth of communion with God.

It is not a matter of finding the time to go off by ourselves to pray and meditate. We must take the time. It may appear to those who need us that we have turned our backs on them and that we have abandoned them. What they may not realize is that unless we go to be alone, unless we take the time to be nourished in prayer and meditation, we will not be able to respond to their needs even if we are with them.

The nature of compassion is not the sharing of ourselves as much as it is the sharing of God through us. When we take the time to come apart and rest awhile, we come to know that it is God who awakens us to the needs around us. It is God who provides the necessary tools with which to meet those needs, and it is God who responds to those needs through us.

Inherent in our compassion is a dynamic force of healing and transformation. It is powerful because it has known powerlessness; it is compassionate because it has known suffering; and it is life-giving because it has known death. This force is tenderness—the gentle, understanding touch of God that emanates from deep within our soul.

Tenderness is that part of us that is hidden under layers of pride, fear, and apathy. It cannot break through our hardness of heart. But life has a way of shattering our most fortified defenses. Tragedies and crises overturn our lives and we are left broken and wounded. The paradox is that it is through the pain and suffering that we are transformed into compassionate beings.

Even through the rubble of our devastation, our tenderness emerges. Whereas before we may not have cared, our experience with pain has opened us to the sensitivity that is within us. Whereas before we may have been obsessed with self-protection, our suffering has left us empathic with the plight of others. Whereas before we may have been rigid in our sense of justice, facing our own mistakes has made us merciful. Now we are closer to the natural state of our humanity: a compassionate, tender-hearted person. "…[B]e kind to one another, tenderhearted…" (Eph 4:32).

Tenderness is more than being fragile or soft; it has to do with deep respect and full appreciation for the well-being of others. Tenderness may be vulnerable, but it is not weak. Its strength comes from its focused and loving attention to the beloved. It has to do with how we treat the ones we love—the ones fate has placed in our circle of life. Do we touch them affectionately to let them know that we cherish them? Do we listen to them fully to let them know we care? Do we encourage them to let them know we are with them? Do we accept them without judging them to let them know that they can come even closer to us? Do we offer them comfort to let them know that we love them?

This is the way of compassionate awareness: to touch, listen, encourage, accept, and comfort with an unconditional love that is beyond comprehension. Our divine nature is tender, not judging; tender, not punishing; tender, not demanding; tender, not manipulating; tender, not intimidating.

The tenderness of God can be felt in the softness of a baby's cheek, as well as through the gentle touch of a friend's hand on our shoulder when we are sad. It can be smelled in the fragrance of spring flowers, as well as in the bowl of soup prepared especially for us by a nurturing mother. It can be seen in the soothing glow of a harvest moon, as well as in the consistent presence of someone who is willing to stay with us through a difficult time. It can be heard in the babbling waters of a mountain brook, as well as in the comforting voice of one who says, "I am here. Don't be afraid."

CHAPTER TEN

Compassionate Action

"Be merciful, just as your Father is merciful."
—Luke 6:36

To be compassionate means to suffer with others. This means that we enter fully and intimately into their lives, including their lowest moments. We identify with the plight of others and are compelled to act on their behalf.

To be compassionate as God is compassionate is to become one with the world, to feel its pulse, and to enter into its passion. But our compassion goes beyond the fire in our heart. It is more than sentiment. It is the force that propels us into action, however grand or modest. It is living interdependently with all living beings, and understanding that we are all intricately involved with one another.

It was late at night and my sister Mary was preparing for bed. As she drank a glass of water, she looked out the kitchen window and saw her neighbor walking down the street with two large baskets of laundry. He was heading for the laundromat that was a mile and a half away. Mary felt badly for him because she knew that he had recently lost his wife to cancer and had two little ones at home. On top of that, his car was not working. She tried to go to sleep but could not. She kept thinking of her neighbor trekking the long distance with his load. She got up, dressed, and drove to find her neighbor. She picked him up and drove him to and from the laundromat. It took a while, but when she finally went to bed she slept well. She had been moved by compassion to leave her comfort in order to help carry the burden of her neighbor.

It is not enough for us to visit the place of suffering in which others live. True compassion compels us to leave the comfort and security of our familiar surroundings and begin to live where others are forced to live.

Through us, the power of compassion soothes the wounds of those around us, mends their broken hearts, and gives them a sense of significance and belonging. Through us, the power of compassion opens the door to understanding, invites peace, and brings harmony in the midst of dissension. The well-being of others is as important to us as our own, and their happiness is also ours. It is as important to stay with their joy as it is to stay with their grief.

Compassion is a gift we share with others. It cannot be induced from without or manipulated externally. Although compassion is a response to the needs of others, it is an action of the heart, not a reaction to the machinations of others.

We see through false happiness and false suffering. For example, we feel no joy for the man who is experiencing the superficial and temporal pleasures of his vices, but we feel compassion toward him because he has put his heart into that which will destroy him. We do not feel compassion for the woman who is complaining over a scratched fender, but we do feel joy for her because this is her worst problem this day.

Of course, in order to see through the false happiness and suffering of others, we must first see through our own false happiness and suffering. For instance, when we are unhappy because we have not gotten our way, this is false suffering. When we are happy because we have gotten our way, this is false happiness.

In compassionate awareness, we respond from the depth of our being to the depth of being of others. It is not a superficial or sentimental reaction to suffering that we offer, but a sincere and soul-felt empathy. Compassionate awareness exists only in the realm of ultimate reality.

It is believed by some that those who have suffered in childhood and who have not been shown compassion are incapable of compassion.

But deeper than the hardened veneer of a life scarred with neglect and abuse is a person's ability to be compassionate to oneself and to others.

Compassion brings with it its own power, regardless of external circumstances. We do not need power to be compassionate, but we need compassion to be powerful. One obvious example of this is Jesus on the cross. His circumstances certainly made him powerless, but his compassion made him powerful, even as he was crucified. What power to be able to pray for the forgiveness of those who are going to kill you, even as they are killing you.

Another example of the power of compassion in the midst of powerlessness has to do with a friend of mine, Sr. Ave Clark. One day Sr. Ave was stopped at a train crossing waiting for a train to pass. Instead of passing, the train left the tracks and crashed into her car, leaving her severely injured. She was taken to the hospital by an ambulance that also carried a rabbi who likewise had been injured by the runaway train. In the ambulance, Sr. Ave was barely conscious, but she heard the rabbi cry out in pain. Through her own agony and confusion, she was compassionately aware enough to comfort the rabbi, telling him that she would pray for him. The rabbi was quoted in the newspaper afterward saying that this compassionate gesture by Sr. Ave let him know that he was not alone in this hour of agony and incertitude.

Compassionate connections are made when and where we least expect. We may receive the compassionate gestures of a friend or family member, and we may also receive them from a total stranger. We may be moved to compassion for victims of a natural disaster far away or we may be overwhelmed by compassion for someone in our own home. Compassion brings its power to bear at times and places of its own choosing. We do not move compassion, rather, it moves us. All we can do is be ready to respond.

The only motivation for true compassion is love. In compassion, we free ourselves from the constraints of our ego and personality and, instead, respond to the suffering of others from our essence. In compassion, we approach each moment of life with acute awareness and loving purpose.

We cannot always measure compassion through our behavior. We must also look to the state of our heart and mind. Those of us who act benevolently or who make great sacrifices for others may or may not be motivated by love. Sometimes what we want is recognition, appreciation, acceptance, or control.

In compassionate awareness, we value the other, not for the way in which the other can meet our needs, but as one who has inherent value. Compassion disallows any concern we might entertain about our personal helplessness. The moment we feel badly because we are powerless to alleviate the suffering of others, we move from compassion and into the realm of the self-centered ego.

There is a difference between our feeling helpless to relieve the suffering of others and being with them in their suffering, even if we cannot relieve it. In the first instance, the concern is about us. That is, we feel badly because we are not able to change things for others. Compassion has more to do with what others are going through, and less with how their situation is affecting us. Sometimes we feel guilty because there is so much suffering in the world that we are powerless to affect. This guilt is not the same as compassion; it has more to do with our ego.

In compassion, once we become aware of the suffering of others, we explore possible ways in which we may help, but even if we cannot, we are constantly mindful of their suffering as if it were our own, which ultimately it is. Being with others in body, mind, and spirit is a constant whether or not we are able to help.

In compassionate awareness, we draw from our own life experience in order to better relate to the experience of others. But there is a big difference between empathizing with others because our experience is similar and projecting our experience onto them. It is important to remember that no two experiences are alike and that, no matter how well we can relate, we do not understand exactly what others are experiencing.

In compassionate awareness, the ego is set aside and, without an active ego, we do not feel either superior or inferior to others. This frees us to deal authentically and at parity with them. We put ourselves in the place of another. We are no longer ourselves alone, but also the other. This is the communion of love.

CHAPTER ELEVEN

The Compassion of Jesus

...he had compassion for them...

—Matthew 9:36

ompassion was at the foundation of all that Jesus taught. His Golden Rule was based on compassion, as were his teachings on forgiveness, mercy, and not judging others. Above all, Jesus taught through example that compassion moves us to act on behalf of those in need.

He taught that responding to the needs of other human beings was tantamount to responding to the needs of God. "Truly I tell you, just as you did it to one of the least of these who are members of my family, you did it to me" (Matt 25:40). The theme that permeated the life and teachings of Jesus was that of oneness. When one of us suffers, we all suffer; when one of us rejoices, we all rejoice. But Jesus went even further. He believed that what happens to creation happens to the Creator. God feels the pain of every being and God feels the joy as well. God receives the blows we inflict on a being and the tender treatment too. Our deeds are done in heaven as they are on earth.

In his parables Jesus spoke often of the power of compassion. He told of the good Samaritan who cared for the stranger, "...a Samaritan while traveling came near him; and when he saw him, he was moved with pity" (Luke 10:33). Jesus called his followers to radical compassion. For him, it was not just about being nice to those who are nice to us. It was about being conscious of what is going on around us and going out of our way to respond to the needs of others. It was about overcoming social pressures and expectations and doing the right thing according to the dictates of the heart. It doesn't matter whether the person who is suffering lives next door to us or comes from a country far away. It doesn't matter whether the person in need believes as we do or not. The only thing that matters is that we be aware, that we be compassionate, and that we respond.

He told of the prodigal son, "...while he was still far off, his father saw him and was filled with compassion; he ran and put his arms around him and kissed him" (Luke 15:20). The constant theme of Jesus' teachings was the power of compassion to break through the walls of resentment, anger, apathy, and hate. It was not pity that Jesus felt for others; it was love. From love comes compassion and from compassion comes forgiveness and reconciliation.

For Jesus, it did not matter how far astray a person went. It did not matter how many laws were broken or how many bridges were burned. It was never too late to make a return.

When Jesus called on his followers to "be merciful, just as your Father is merciful" (Luke 6:36), he was asking them for much more than virtuous comportment. He was proposing a way of life that was expansive, life-giving, nurturing, and healing. He believed that a life lived from compassion was a life grounded in God. Jesus knew that to be compassionate we must first be awake and aware of the life around us. He knew that to be compassionate we must be willing to enter fully into our humanity and the humanity of others. He asked his followers to be as God is, but he knew this was impossible without first communing with God in prayer and meditation.

Perhaps the strongest plea that Jesus made for compassion was his admonition, "You shall love your neighbor as yourself" (Matt 22:39). To love another as oneself necessitates setting aside divisiveness and embracing the reality of oneness. Jesus knew that we cannot love others unless we love ourselves and, consequently, we cannot be compassionate toward others if we are not compassionate toward ourselves.

Jesus did not just teach compassion, he lived it. "...[H]e had compassion for them, because they were like sheep without a shepherd..." (Mark 6:34). He responded compassionately to the needs of the lost by offering himself as a shepherd they could follow.

With a maternal instinct, Jesus tended to those who were scattered and discouraged. "Jerusalem, Jerusalem….How often have I desired to gather your children together as a hen gathers her brood under her wings…" (Matt 23:37). As only a mother can, Jesus would sacrifice everything, even his life, for the sake of those for whom he had such great love and compassion.

Moved by compassion, Jesus offered comfort to those weighed down by the vicissitudes of life, "Come to me, all you that are weary and are carrying heavy burdens, and I will give you rest. Take my yoke upon you, and learn from me; for I am gentle and humble in heart, and you will find rest for your souls. For my yoke is easy, and my burden is light" (Matt 11:28–30). He would offer himself as a companion on the difficult road of life. He would help carry the burden, he would set the example of humility, and he would give respite to the soul.

Jesus had a visceral reaction to the suffering he witnessed all around him. He was moved to compassion and compelled to act on behalf of others. He saw people hungry, "I have compassion for the crowd, because they…have nothing to eat" (Mark 8:2), and he did something about it. Whether offering physical or spiritual nourishment, Jesus was a man of action. His mind knew that there were limits to what he could do for others, but his spirit moved him beyond those limits. His great compassion for the plight of others, coupled with his radical faith in God's love working through him, empowered him to heal others in myriad ways.

He beheld a people blind to the ways of God and his heart broke with sadness: "Moved with compassion, Jesus touched their eyes. Immediately they regained their sight and followed him" (Matt 20:34). Just as Jesus shared the pain of life with others, he also wanted to share with them the joy of knowing God. He gave sight to the blind with his actions and his words.

When Jesus saw his close friends sorrowfully weeping over the death of their brother, "...he was greatly disturbed in spirit and deeply moved..." (John 11:33). "Jesus began to weep" (John 11:35). He was greatly affected by what he witnessed and was not afraid to feel emotion. He was angered by hypocrisy, frustrated by faithlessness, saddened by apathy, indignant over injustice, and bereaved over loss. He saw no inconsistency between being a man of faith and feeling deeply about the suffering that he witnessed in the world.

The compassion of Jesus was the compassion of God. When he healed the sick, he would charge them afterward, "...tell them how much the Lord has done for you, and what mercy he has shown you" (Mark 5:19). Jesus saw himself as the way, the hand, the instrument of God in the world.

CHAPTER TWELVE

Instrument of God

Lord, make me an instrument of your peace.
                                    —St. Francis of Assisi

S t. Francis of Assisi prayed constantly to be used by God. His prayer epitomizes the essence of compassionate awareness. Francis was, above all, continually conscious of God, of others, and of nature. He saw himself as a conduit for the love of God in the world.

Make me an instrument of your peace. All peace emanates from the presence of God and our compassionate soul is the presence of God in the world. As a paintbrush becomes one with the artist, so we become one with God as we tend to creation.

Where there is hatred, let me sow love. There will be hatred in the world, even in our heart, yet love is stronger than hatred and is everlasting. Even in a field that is covered with the weeds of hatred that choke off life, the seed of love can be sown. It dies into the ground then bursts forth to flourish and proliferate. Our compassionate soul tills the hardened soil and prepares it to receive the seed. The tilling is prayer and meditation.

Where there is injury, pardon. Our compassionate soul is first of all forgiving. In this state of mind and heart, we are willing to forgive those who have injured us and others. We are also willing to forgive ourselves for injuries we have caused. Our compassionate soul is merciful toward the whole world. Instead of allowing one injury to beget another, we allow pardon to beget pardon.

Where there is doubt, faith. Our compassionate soul allows others to be real; this means that we accept their doubtfulness as well as their faithfulness. After all, doubt is not the opposite of faith, nor is it less than faith. Doubt is a state of uncertainty about something; it opens us up to possibilities that we have not considered. Then, in faith, possibilities become beliefs by which we can chart our course in life.

Where there is despair, hope. Our compassionate soul does not discount the despair that is felt by others. Instead, we allow the despair and even empathize with it. At the same time, we introduce possibilities and alternatives to staying in the desperate state. We can relate to the desperation, but we can also relate to the glimmer of hope that abides in every soul.

Where there is darkness, light. It is not so much that darkness must be eliminated by light, but that darkness must be embraced as an integral part of life. It is through the darkness that we discover the light and it is the light within that enables us to endure the darkness when it comes. Our compassionate soul enters the darkness with others and remains there as long as necessary before we move together into the light.

Where there is sadness, joy. Sadness is a gift from life. It is our human response to loss and misfortune. Our compassionate soul allows the sadness of others and enters into it with them. Because we dare to share in their sadness, we can also participate in their joy.

Grant that I may not so much seek to be consoled, as to console. As our compassionate soul is moved to console a broken heart, we remember our own times of sorrow. Because we are one with those we console, we too benefit from that consolation.

To be understood, as to understand. We all want desperately to be understood. But sometimes our desire to be understood blinds us to the reality of others. Our compassionate soul can pay full attention to others only when we have first paid attention to God in prayer and meditation.

To be loved, as to love. The more we seek love for ourselves, the more it eludes us. But when our compassionate soul gives love to others, love returns to us. Although we do not love in order to be loved, when we dare to love, we begin a chain reaction in the world.

For it is in giving that we receive. Our compassionate soul lives to give and gives to live.

It is in pardoning that we are pardoned. Our compassionate soul clings to nothing.

It is in dying that we are born to eternal life. Our compassionate soul dies into life.

For the Sake of God

We are the incarnation.

We, the hands and feet of God, are the hope of the world.

We are in God and God is in us.

God, who dwells in us, can speak our words if we allow it.

God, who believes in us, can work through us if we permit it.

We receive the peace of God, not the external peace of the world, but the peace that calms the storm in our heart and pacifies the warfare in our mind.

Let all that we think, all that we feel, and all that we do, be for the sake of God.

Let our love for God be paramount; let it be the force behind our life. We cannot see the spirit of the God we follow, yet it abides in us always. It comforts us and teaches us; it shows itself to the eyes of our soul.

CHAPTER THIRTEEN

Spirit of Equality

The LORD is good to all,
and his compassion is over all that
he has made.
—Psalm 145:9

E ach encounter with another person is unique because each person is unique. Respect for who the other person is and for that person's reality is paramount in our compassionate response.

Compassionate awareness brings with it the spirit of equality. We do not charge in like the cavalry ready to rescue those in distress. We do not take over to solve their problems; instead, our authentic and empathetic response is to enter into the problem with them.

This lesson was brought home to me recently as I tried to help my ninety-two-year-old mother deal with her dementia. I was very clear about what I thought she needed in order to be happy and healthy, and I tried to impose my ideas on her.

Rationally, I knew that what I was suggesting to her was better for her, but I had forgotten that what I believed to be right, is not always what is best for others. I had left out of the equation the things that mattered most to her, whether I thought they should matter or not. I was being helpful, but certainly not compassionate. I was being for her but not with her. When we act from compassion, we respond to the whole person, including the person's physical, psychological, and spiritual needs.

In compassion, our own agendas and time tables are set aside and our expectations are diminished. We may be clinging to a particular personal view of things, but in compassionate awareness, our mind and heart are opened to new and varying perspectives. To be with others compassionately requires that we be with who they are, how they are, and when they are.

In compassionate awareness, we do not confuse pity with compassion. Pity separates, compassion unites; pity differentiates, compassion assimilates. Pity observes the suffering of others from a detached and distant place, compassion experiences the suffering of others up close and personal as one's own. Pity is felt among unequals, while compassion requires equality.

Compassion goes beyond mere sympathy or a sentimental attachment. It is more than feeling sorry for someone and reaching down to give them a hand. It is not enough to just throw them a lifeline from the safe and secure shore. In compassionate awareness, we dive into the murky waters of life and tread there alongside our drowning brothers and sisters. Sometimes we can help them swim ashore; sometimes our compassion is limited to sharing in their helplessness.

Compassion goes beyond the awareness or acknowledgment of the hurt of others; it compels us to enter into the abyss of pain and sorrow. It brings us into the hurt that we may share it. Sometimes our compassion moves us to action, but often it has more to do with sharing a common helplessness and just being with them during their distress. Sometimes our compassion may appear useless. It may seem weak instead of strong and vulnerable instead of in control.

In compassion, we bear witness to what is. We are there to see it, feel it, and experience it. We do not offer to others theories or concepts about life and living; rather, we offer the benefit of our own life experience. Those of us who have suffered greatly and therefore understand the nature of suffering first hand reach a deeper level of compassion toward others who suffer. Having ourselves moved through grief, we know the devastation that loss leaves in its wake. Having been broken, we understand the broken hearted. Having experienced loneliness, we can empathize with the lonely.

We too shed the tears that come from the eyes of the miserable; we too wait through the long night with those who feel alone, and mourn with the bereaved. In compassion, we create an environment in which others may feel nurtured and supported. We provide them a safe holding environment.

We can be patient without being compassionate, but we cannot be compassionate without being patient. In compassionate awareness, we slow down and wait for others. This is equally true with children, the elderly, the infirmed, and the disabled. To slow down and wait means that we are willing to adjust our pace to that of others. We patiently adapt our steps to those of little children as we guide them by the hand. We move patiently according to the gait of elderly persons, lest we cause them to fall. We listen carefully and patiently to every word that comes from the mouths of speech-impaired persons so that they may be understood. We willingly, cheerfully, and patiently tend to the needs of such persons, even when they are demanding and difficult.

Compassion is based on both unification and differentiation. In compassion we recognize our union with others, but this unity does not consume them. Instead, we respect their otherness and encourage their individual completion.

Our compassion is balanced between two extremes. When we separate ourselves too much from others, we lose touch with them. When we enmesh ourselves in the lives of others, we lose ourselves in them. In either case, we are not in a position to help them or ourselves.

We can direct, guide, and mentor others to conform to our expectations of how they should live their lives. We can mold their minds and condition their behavior toward becoming better persons. We can teach them, inspire them, and boost their self-esteem. All this we can do, but we must not call it compassion.

We watch ourselves interact with others, being mindful of the way in which we treat them and of the words with which we choose to communicate. We are conscious of others, of their needs, of their pains, and of their circumstances. We are awake and present to them. We look at them and listen to their words with total attention.

CHAPTER FOURTEEN

Listening Heart

Hear my prayer, O LORD,
and give ear to my cry...
—Psalm 39:12

To listen compassionately to others is one of the greatest gifts we can give to them. To be truly heard by another human being validates our life experience and makes our suffering bearable.

We all need to be reflected on the compassionate heart of another person. It seems there is no suffering that is beyond our endurance, and no condition with which we cannot cope, as long as our anguish can be expressed to another, and heard.

What a life-giving experience it is to be listened to. It is as though we are hearing ourselves through the ears of another. Someone who wants to listen to us with no agenda but to hear us is truly a blessing of life. Can anyone bestow on us greater gifts than a listening ear and a responding heart?

Telling someone, either verbally or nonverbally, that we are feeling hurt, sad, depressed, angry, or otherwise wounded, puts our emotion out where we can better deal with it. Having that emotion mirrored back to us by a person who has heard it, gives us an even better grasp of it. Even more, as our emotion is heard and acknowledged by another, we feel as though we are significant enough in life to be taken seriously, and cared for enough by another to be listened to.

Children, especially, need to be heard regardless of what they are saying. I have witnessed parents who are very focused on teaching their children to be good citizens, but who pay little or no attention to them. I have been in classrooms in which teachers insist that students pay attention to what is being taught, but who fail to pay attention to the personal expressions of the students. In other words, both parents and teachers miss a great opportunity to listen and be compassionately present to the children. When they are, the result is that children not only become good citizens, but they also become healthier persons; they not only learn content, but they also learn to appreciate themselves and others. A child who is listened to by adults grows up feeling worthwhile and capable of contributing to the world. In turn, that child as an adult will listen to others, including children.

Listening means so much more than registering sounds or processing words through the mind. It means opening ourselves up to another person in such a way that he or she is what matters most at that moment. Listening means that we let go of our own noises and distractions, if only for a moment, in order to really hear what the other person is saying to us. It means not getting stuck on the definition of the words used, but going beyond the words to the feelings they are attempting to express.

When we listen with our heart, we hear not only what emanates from the mouth of a person, but also the silent language of the body and the revealing gestures of the face. It means noting the different intonations of the voice, and recognizing the hidden messages that are sometimes veiled in jest or feigned disinterest. Because the person to whom we are listening is also watching us, it is important that our body language conveys interest, availability, and concern.

My eyes were filled with tears and my face was buried in my hands. I could not see my therapist to whom I was relating a painful experience, but I knew he was there and I knew he was listening to me. I knew because even as I was talking between sobs, I heard him utter a deep and compassionate sigh. Instantly I felt validated, affirmed, and heard. It is hard to believe that a single sigh could have such effect, but of course it was much more than a sigh. It was a spontaneous and natural response to what he was hearing. It was a physical reaction that carried with it a powerful psychological impact. Even words of understanding and support would not have been as helpful to me at that time.

In my own psychotherapy practice I listen to myself even as I listen to the client. It is not that I divide my attention between my client and myself; rather, I listen to both of us at the same time. I am aware of the client's words and gestures and of the words that are not said, as well as the impact the client's words are having on my psyche. I notice, for example, if I am being emotionally triggered by something the client has said or if my counter-transference is interfering with the therapy. Dual listening is not limited to the therapeutic setting. Listening to ourselves as we listen to others is not a distraction. On the contrary, it is a way of staying clear of distractions and focused on what is being said to us.

Compassionate listening requires that we be less engaged in dialogue and more openly receptive to the thoughts and emotions that are being entrusted to us. Sometimes an occasional question is in order, usually not. A nodding head or a gentle invitation to "say more about that," is all that is needed to continue the flow of self-disclosure. The person to whom we are listening knows whether or not we are really listening. They can tell by observing our eye contact, our body language, and our general attentiveness.

It is so amazing how being listened to by another person lightens our burden. Although all the love in the world will not eliminate the suffering that abounds around us, through compassionate listening we can be for one another even through the suffering.

It is equally important that we listen to ourselves. We listen to the voice within; it speaks to us of our nature. It tells us the truth to which we must respond.

We listen to the pleading of our body. It is racked with pain and twisted by tension. It is wounded by disease and broken by neglect. It asks for rest and relaxation for it is weary from overwork and underplay. It asks to be touched and it asks to be healed. We hear its plea to stop the abuse. We hear its cry for tender care and loving attention. We listen to the voice of our physical self; it calls us toward wholeness.

We listen to the whispers of our mind. We can hear them only if we ignore the intrusion of vagabond thoughts and the distraction of wild imaginings. We hear the voice that comes from the reservoir of all experience and knowledge, of all the past and possibility. This is the voice of wisdom that will guide us through the desert. It will tell us what works best for us, and it will help us set priorities. This is the voice that will help us make decisions all the moments of our life. We listen to the voice of our mind. Its promptings will feed our creativity and its questions will explore great mysteries.

We listen to the music of our heart. Its notes are sweet and gentle, harsh and explosive. Its range is from high and ecstatic to low and depressive. Its melody is sometimes sad and at other times pregnant with the joy of heaven. The music of our heart sings the song of our emotions. Its lyrics tell us how we are responding to the reality of life. We listen to the words and we listen to the music; we know what we are feeling and sing it to another. We do not critique the music of our heart. We just let it be heard.

We listen to the silence of our spirit. It is here that our whole self can rest in unconditional acceptance and nurturing love. Here the quest for knowing gives way to the security of believing. Here is where our scattered emotions settle into the peace of oneness. We listen to the silence of our spirit. It invites us to integrate the worlds of our body, mind, and heart into the wholeness of God. It tells us that it is through the totality of our humanity that we transcend it. Amid the silence of our spirit we will hear the sounds of faith, hope, and love. We will hear the sounds of life, and more, we will hear the still small voice of God.

CHAPTER FIFTEEN

Compassionate Presence

"I am deeply grieved, even to death; remain here,
and stay awake with me."   —Matthew 26:38

Jesus knew that the Messianic name *Immanuel*
meant "God is with us." He believed God was
transcendent, but also immanent. He understood that compassion meant to be with, and he
promised others his perpetual presence whether in
person or in spirit. "And remember, I am with you
always, to the end of the age" (Matt 28:20).

But in his greatest need, Jesus could not
count on his friends to be with him. In the garden
of Gethsemane Jesus was sorrowful unto death and
asked his disciples to stay with him. "Then he came
to the disciples and found them sleeping; and he
said to Peter, 'So, could you not stay awake with me
one hour? Stay awake and pray that you may not
come into the time of trial; the spirit indeed is willing, but the flesh is weak" (Matt 26:40–41).

Even with crisis breaking all around them, Jesus' disciples were asleep, oblivious to what was happening in the moment. Jesus needed them awake and present to him, but their temptation was to be unconscious, unavailable to life.

"I am deeply grieved, even to death; remain here, and stay awake with me" (Matt 26:38). These are the desperate words Jesus spoke to his friends as he faced inevitable suffering and death. They are also the words that we have heard from a friend or family member in the midst of crisis. They are words we probably have spoken ourselves as we reached out from the pit of our despair.

How comforting it is to have someone stay with us when we are experiencing the darkness that sometimes comes in life. How encouraging to know that we are not alone through our ordeal. Sometimes having someone there with us makes the difference between hope and despair. Just their compassionate presence is sufficient to get us through the night. We are in need of compassionate presence from others. It is the salve that soothes us and the nourishment that helps us grow.

Those who dare to stay with us do not necessarily solve our problems or relieve our pain, but their commitment to be with us and offer their care and concern helps us to cope with whatever is to come. There is more to the ministry of compassion than just staying with those in need. It calls us to remain and stay awake. That is, we must let them know that we are also keeping vigil with them through the long and difficult hours. Through our compassion, we enter into the valley of shadows with them. Through love we attend to them and give them someone to hold.

We remain and stay awake when we sit and listen to a grieving mother as she tells her story one more time, and when we kneel to pray with a friend who faces tumultuous times, or when we hold the hand of someone who is sinking into the depths of depression.

But it is not easy to remain and stay awake with those in need. The spirit indeed is willing, but the flesh is weak. The scene in the garden of Gethsemane is not unlike the scene in the lives of many of us who are tempted by distractions and become unconscious to our lives and the lives of others. We are so easily pulled away by other interests and obligations. It is difficult because sometimes we are not sure what to say or do. Other times we are afraid to face our own vulnerability or to be exposed to a sad environment lest it be contagious.

Sometimes we are impatient and want to get on with our own lives. Sometimes we are just plain lazy or tired and fall asleep, or we leave mentally because life in real time is too much for us to take. Sometimes we leave habitually, forgetting that our natural state is to be fully conscious, fully alive, and compassionately aware.

Every moment of our life is precious, whether it is filled with ecstasy or agony, blessedness or misery. To stay awake this hour is to receive with gratitude God's gift of life. But it is hard to stay awake. Thoughts sneak into our mind and emotions capture our attention. Worry is a great temptation for us because it gives us a false sense of control. Sometimes we consciously choose unconsciousness through aimless and mindless behavior.

The temptations that take us away from the eternal now also come in the form of lamentations about something that happened in the past or anxieties about what might happen in the future. In either case, we abandon the present. We may fantasize about what could be, even as we ignore what is.

Left to distraction, our mind becomes preoccupied with meaningless thoughts that lead to judgmentalism, envy, anger, hurt, and other emotions that only disturb our peace and the peace of others. Unconsciously, we wander off into the far country of unrealities where we encounter the illusions of separateness and self-sufficiency.

Sometimes compassionate awareness is hard on us. It is not always pleasant to enter into the world of others. We can be excited with a friend for the promotion she just received, and we can rejoice with our sibling for the good news he heard from his doctor. But it's more difficult to feel with a friend in the midst of her grief or a family member who is terrified about his son's drug abuse problem. Our temptation is to run away from such suffering. It takes a lot of practice to remain in compassionate presence.

To simply be brought down by the depressed mood of another person is not empathy, much less compassion. Instead of being consumed by the emotional state of another person, we must be like the lifeguard who plunges into the water to save a drowning person, but not without first getting the necessary grounding to avert being drowned by the person in peril.

If we are overly attached, hostile, or indifferent toward others, we cannot be compassionate toward them because we are too focused on ourselves. As we enter into compassionate awareness, we enter into a state of equanimity with all that is, including ourselves. With an open heart and mind we allow ourselves to get to know others. In this way we dissolve attachment, hostility, and indifference.

Sometimes it seems as if our compassion is in conflict with itself. We may be moved to respond compassionately to one situation while at the same time be moved to respond compassionately to a completely different situation. Here we need to recognize and accept our limitations. In humility, we admit to ourselves that we cannot be in two places at the same time and that we have limited resources from which to draw. Our compassion may be for both sets of circumstances, but our immediate compassionate response must be to only one. Compassion compels us to give our full attention to whom and what is before us and not to be divided between here and there.

CHAPTER SIXTEEN

Angels Came

The angel said to her, "Do not be afraid…"
—Luke 1:30

"Angeling" is the ministry of compassion. It is the manifestation of God's love working through our lives.

At some point in our lives we all encounter a painful and frightening time that tries us to the breaking point. It is best if we do not embark on this journey alone. Oh, that we would always have a compassionate angel by our side as we face the dark nights of our soul—someone who would see us through the difficult process of growth, and would guide us through the steps.

An angel is, above all, someone who stays with us when things get tough, someone who helps us to bring forth something from within ourselves, someone who understands the process we must undergo and allays our fears. An angel can be a woman or a man, as long as she or he is willing to be there with us through our ordeal. One need not be a nun, minister, or priest, counselor or nurse, teacher or sponsor, although these people may serve as angels. One need only be a caring friend who holds us when we need to be held; who listens to us when we need to talk; and who guides us when we need to learn. An angel is, above all, a person of compassion, willing to enter into our pain. It is a person who is grounded in practicality and reality, yet allows the force of irrationality and mysticism to have its way as well.

An angel is someone we can trust to keep our best interest at heart; someone to whom we can turn in our darkest hour for a word of encouragement and a sign of understanding. An angel walks with us through the confusing maze of life, and coaches us to persevere as we encounter trouble, resistance, and the anxiety that comes with change. An angel inspires us to tap the courage from within that helps us to move ahead despite our fear.

The compassion of others can see us through the most somber times of our life. The tragic death of my son brought in its wake a wave of overwhelming compassion. In the midst of this unexplainable storm, I saw glimpses of God, who is love. This unbearable tragedy brought about, if only for a little while, a gathering of angels. They began to come in the early hours of the tragedy. The priest who loves beyond measure came not only to console, but also to enter into the suffering himself. He would stay with us throughout the ordeal. The angels came in the form of friends bearing gifts of food to nourish and strengthen us. They offered a shoulder on which to cry. They mixed their tears with ours.

They didn't take away our agony or even ease our pain, but they loved enough to stay with us and share in our suffering. These compassionate friends had come to be with us for three days of torturous waiting before our son died from the injuries of a car accident. They had come knowing that they would be able to do little to change the course of events, yet wanting to be with us in those moments of deep distress.

Of course none of them could feel the pain in the same way that we did, but they dared to get as close to our pain as they could. Their compassion took them to the scene of suffering. They weren't satisfied to send condolences from afar. Once there, they entered into the feelings that filled the room: pain, fear, confusion, brokenness, anguish, hope.

In compassionate presence they were crying with us, waiting powerlessly with us for what was to come. They immersed themselves in our hour of agony. Normally, we try to avoid pain. Why would these men and women enter into it voluntarily?

During the wait, the colors of compassion were many splendored. One man allowed himself to mentally put his son in my son's deathbed so he could empathize as much as a father could. A woman sighed deeply as she looked into my eyes. I knew she was with me in my helplessness. One person wept, another prayed, while yet another put his arm around my drooping shoulders.

They remembered that in moments of pain and suffering, it is not advice that is needed or even words of hope and reassurance. The grief we shared made us one in spirit and words seemed only to get in the way. What really makes a difference in our hour of need is that someone remain here and stay awake with us. Although there was nothing that could be said or done, these friends and neighbors, these angels, were there for us.

In this dark, dark time of my life it was hard to believe in anything, yet, I did believe in God, I did believe in love, and I did believe in angels. I still believe in angels, not those winged beings dressed in flowing gowns and radiating light. Rather, I mean those grounded beings dressed in ordinary clothing, radiating love and compassion as they enter and leave us. I believe in angels who offer us hope when we despair, guidance when we are lost, and encouragement when we are down. There are angels who give us strength when we are weak, protection when we are vulnerable, and who help us carry our burden when we can bear no more. Angels help us gain clarity and insight, and they give us the courage to learn and grow, even through the pain. Angels give us womb-space to rest, to be, and to flourish.

The Hebrew word for compassion, *rachamim,* is derived from the word for the womb of Yahweh. It is through this womb-love that we come to know the compassion of God. The womb is the place of propagation, generation, gestation, and animation. In the womb, life is received and held protectively until the time of birthing, then the womb moves life into the world.

The Womb of God

You are born of the womb of God.
From depths divine you emanate,
from the fountain of life you flow.
Yours is the nature of Mother God,
yours is the way of love.

You are entrusted to be the Life,
to touch the world, to heal the
    brokenness.
You, who are grounded in reality,
are strength and courage,
wisdom and compassion.

You are the face of God.
From your eyes comes the light of
    consciousness,
from your mouth, the song of the soul.
Heaven and earth converge in your
    bosom.
Hallowed be your compassionate
    heart.

ILLUMINATIONBOOKS

Other Books in the Series

Little Pieces of Light...Darkness and Personal Growth
by Joyce Rupp

Appreciating God's Creation Through Scripture
by Alice L. Laffey

Let Yourself Be Loved
by Phillip Bennett

Living Simple in an Anxious World
by Robert J. Wicks

A Rainy Afternoon with God
by Catherine B. Cawley

God Lives Next Door
by Lyle K. Weiss

Hear the Just Word & Live It
by Walter J. Burghardt, SJ

The Love That Keeps Us Sane
by Marc Foley, OCD

The Threefold Way of Saint Francis
by Murray Bodo, OFM

Everyday Virtues
by John W. Crossin, OSFS

The Mysteries of Light
by Roland J. Faley, TOR

Healing Mysteries
by Adrian Gibbons Koester

Carrying the Cross with Christ
by Joseph T. Sullivan

Saintly Deacons
by Deacon Owen F. Cumming

Finding God Today
by E. Springs Steele

Hail Mary and Rhythmic Breathing
by Richard Galentino

The Eucharist
by Joseph M. Champlin

Gently Grieving
by Constance M. Mucha

Devotions for Caregivers
by Marilyn Driscoll

Be a Blessing
by Elizabeth M. Nagel

The Art of Affirmation
by Robert Furey

Jesus' Love Stories
by John F. Loya & Joseph A. Loya